Unbroken

Kamaliha Brewster
Unbroken

Published by Spines
ISBN: 979-8-89569-804-4

Unbroken

A Story of Betrayal, Resilience, and Healing

Kamaliha Brewster

Contents

Chapter 1
A Story of Family, Abuse, and Self-Discovery

The unthinkable things that have happened in my life are beyond disbelief. I believe that all my trials and tribulations have occurred because God wanted me to learn my own strength, build up my confidence, and overcome the challenges that I endured. I want to tell you about some of the things that I encountered growing up and how my family treated me. I was born in the hot summer of July and my mother wanted me to have a name with a meaning. I was the only child, and her only daughter was born at 9 pounds and 10 ounces. A bundle of joy to my mother and she spoiled me rotten with a lot of clothes, and toys, and took me on trips out of town with her and my dad. At the age of four years old, I was molested by a male cousin who was 18 years old. This went on for a while at my grandma's house until one day my cousin Terrell walked into the room and told me to get dressed. I did what he said put on my clothes and walked out of the room. My cousin asked me," "How long had that been happening?" I said, "A while, a month or two I think." He asked me why I didn't tell anyone. I told him because Reggie said, "He would kill me, and nobody would believe me."

I didn't know it was wrong when I was a child to let someone touch me and do inappropriate things with me. My cousin told my mom and she took me to the doctor. The doctor called the police at her office because my hymen was broken.

My mom went to the police and pressed charges. It broke my family's foundation because, after that happened, my mom had to send me to daycare. She didn't trust her mother or anyone in her family to watch me. My grandma and mom stopped talking for several years. My mom and I went to court, and I told the judge what happened. Reggie was sentenced to prison. The police went to his high school and arrested him on campus. My mom put me in counseling, and my counselor, Bonnie, introduced me to journaling. She also helped me heal the pain from my abuse. She taught me to write down my feelings, whether good or bad, in my journal. I began writing down everything that happened to me, how it traumatized me, and how God let that happen to me. In counseling, I learned that I have to forgive him; God will make him suffer for hurting me and all the pain he caused in my life.

I felt uncomfortable around men and boys for a while. I didn't like it when people touched me, tapped me on my shoulder, stood too close to me, or got in my personal space. It was tragic for me, as a young girl, to have experienced sexual abuse from a family member. My mother's family always treated me like I was the problem or that something was wrong with me. I am an only child, so I always tried to have a bond with my family. The more I tried to gain their love and affection, the more they treated me as the black sheep. Some of my cousins who stayed out of town would always say that I think I'm better than them. It hurt my feelings because, being an only child, I didn't understand why they would treat me differently. We are family, and I was raised to treat everyone with respect and equally.

I couldn't help that my parents worked and made sure I had a place to stay, food to eat, and clothes to wear. Their parents worked too and had food, clothes, and a place for them to stay. I was spoiled. My birthday and Christmas were my favorite holidays. I would receive so many gifts and always got everything I wanted. I remember I wanted a bike, and I had training wheels on it. My uncle Mozell came by to visit my mom and dad. He saw me riding my bike outside and said, "Hey, niece, you're getting so tall now. Don't you think you need to take the training wheels off your bike?" I told him I was afraid I would fall. He said, "No, you won't. You'll just keep riding your bike like you are now." He said to give it a try. I said, "Okay." He went to his car, grabbed a wrench, and removed the training wheels from my bike. My uncle removed the training wheels and said, "Try to ride your bike now." I sat down on my yellow BMX bike, pedaled, went down the driveway, and turned around. I was so shocked that I could ride my BMX bike without falling off.

I went to school and loved to learn new things. My family always makes me feel like I'm an outsider who isn't worthy of love.

Chapter 2
Betrayal, Resilience, and Forgiveness

I am the black sheep, an only child, and very original. My mom instilled in me to love myself and love my name, which means African princess, knowledge, precious one, only daughter, born to wealth. My grandma would make quilts and clothes for people. She told me to always believe in myself and be genuine, even if it's not accepted by others —God sees it. I would sit out on the porch during the summertime and watch the cars go by, talking with my grandma about life. She told me I was an old soul and had always been wise beyond my years. My family would have dinner parties and gatherings where people would eat, drink, dance, play dominoes and cards, and the kids would be playing outside in the yard or in my room. I would play school with my little cousins or my parents' friends. Sometimes I would play board games like Chutes and Ladders,

Uno, and The Game of Life. I miss those times of family gatherings.

I have been betrayed by my cousins. They lied and stole my CDs, jewelry, curling iron, and money. One cousin came to spend the summer with me when I was a child, and when she left, she took my curling iron, bra, and diamond earrings. I have never stolen anything in my life. The summer she visited, I took her around town, sightseeing, and tried to make her visit a fun one. Another cousin stole my CDs. She came by to get some money that my uncle left her, and she came into my bedroom, sat in a chair, went through my purse, and stole my debit card. She did this when I had all four of my wisdom teeth removed. She went to the bank with her friend Chris and stole $5,000 from my bank account. I told my mom, and she wanted to speak with her mom. I was so pissed and wanted to beat her up!

My mom, grandma, and I went over to my cousin's mom's house. She was probably about 15 years old. My grandma, mom, and her mom were discussing things and talking to her. She was looking nonchalant and went outside, so I followed her. I could barely talk with the blood still oozing from my gums. I told her I would whoop her butt if I wasn't in so much pain. She never apologized. I put my hands around her neck and began to choke her. I couldn't believe the person was a family member who I would give money to, took her and her friends around town so they wouldn't have to catch the bus, bought her clothes and shoes, and rewarded her if she made good grades in school.

I went to the police station and pressed charges, and I had to go to my bank to dispute the charges because she stole money and overdrew my account. I called the police department to check on the case, and she had called them, telling the police she was me and wanted to drop the charges. I never called, and I asked the police how they could take a verbal word over the phone. I told them I knew how to deal with her since they couldn't. Another cousin I let move in with me rummaged through all my stuff. I took her to work once she got a job. I bought her clothes from JCPenney so she could visit her kids. She never paid me back but talked about me! Then, she made accusations that I stole her DVD player, cussed me out, and threatened to kill me. I told her over the phone that nobody was scared of her. If you're going to do something, then do it. My dad had her DVD player, and he forgot to give it back to her. She was so high on cocaine, she forgot about it, but she was texting me crazy stuff and calling me about it. She moved back to New Jersey, and I hadn't heard from her in years. When my uncle was ill, I went to visit him, and she stayed with her dad. She forgot about everything she'd done to me but asked me for $10 to wash her clothes and said she would pay me back. But I knew she wouldn't.

Why do I have to be the one who forgives people when they lie, cuss me out, and never apologize for the bull they do? My grandmother always told me that family looks out for each other. Now, don't get me wrong, I love my family, even if they don't love me. I will help anyone in their time of need and will give them my last. I am always called selfish, even by my own mother! I am not selfish, but they have taught me to be selfish because of how they treat me. I don't have such a forgiving heart as Granny. I hold grudges forever. I forgive them, but I just don't mess with them because they will need me before I need them. I always wanted my family to treat me like I treat them. They don't know what I've been through; they just think I am crazy and call me names. They couldn't have dealt with any of the things that I've been through in my life.

I was gang-raped during my teenage years. I joined the military to escape from the pain, but in the service, the men were intimidated because I could do a lot of physical exercise like them, and I passed all of my tests with high scores. So, I was bullied. One day on the ship, someone closed the door but screamed my name, so when I turned around, the cement door hit me in the head. I fell down, had a concussion, and woke up in the hospital. The impact from the door caused me to have a skull fracture, and my migraines are severe. I had a brain tumor for seven years, and with medication, it finally shrunk. I still have migraines every other day. I think I'm like a cat with nine lives—when I was 4 years old, through teenage trauma, the military, an accident on the freeway where I was hit by an 18-wheeler which totaled my dad's car, and when I got pregnant, I had an accident on the 405 freeway where a man ran into the back of my car. My baby was okay, but just the fact that someone didn't want me to have my baby. I always wanted to be married before I had a baby, but my daughter's father promised me he would marry me.

Chapter 3
A Mother's Journey

After my baby was born, he and I started arguing, and he began staying out with his friends, leaving me at home with the baby. My family was all in my business, trying to tell me what I should and shouldn't do in my relationship. I didn't know and thought they had my best interest at heart. My family didn't want to see me happy, and I listened to those miserable people. It ruined my relationship. We broke up, and I became a single mother. Nobody wants to be a single mother, but I was forced to be one. I didn't work for two years and stayed home with my daughter until she could talk.

I was so afraid that someone might try to hurt my daughter, like the things that happened to me. I went back to work when she turned two. I taught my daughter her ABCs, how to count, phonetic sounds, and math, and I had learning videos. We watched Sesame Street.

I gave my family a chance to watch my daughter, and my cousin was being mean and had someone molest my daughter. I will never forgive her for that. I was stalked by my cousin and her friends for three years. I went to the police, and they didn't help. I went to court and put a bond/restraining order on both of them. If I saw them, I was going to beat them up because how could someone be that cruel to my child?

My family had a gathering during the summertime and invited her. I asked them if she was coming because, if so, my daughter and I weren't coming. They invited her and made me feel so uncomfortable. I will never forgive my mom and family for that. I told them I disown all of them, and I meant it.

I am the only child and have no problem being without family or friends. I can be by myself, and it's okay. If I want to go to a movie or travel, I can go by myself or with my child. I have been betrayed by everyone I trusted!

I have one friend who steals my ideas. If I say I want to get this dream car, she will go get it before me. If I have a business idea, she will do it before I do it. I'm not mad because I should have kept it to myself and not told her. I procrastinate, and at first, I was hurt, but now I just realize I have some great ideas, and so she uses them. Maybe I should have charged her for using my ideas, but no, I am happy for her.

I am not mad, jealous, or envious of anyone. I am happy for them. I have been single because I'd rather focus on my daughter and myself until I meet the man God has sent to me. I am not settling for a man just so I won't be single anymore. I know my worth and can be myself because I love myself! People will think I'm jealous, but I am not.

Chapter 4
The Heartbreaking Truth of My Family's Struggles

I miss my three uncles, grandma, cousin, and aunt who have passed away. They were always there when I was feeling down. They knew just what to say to make me cheer up. I can be depressed at times, but hell, look at all that I went through. My family was my downfall because I allowed them to hurt me. I would love to trace my roots to see where I truly come from. My grandfather had land, and his family were cowboys, farmers, and craftsmen. My grandma was a seamstress, a nurse, and a godly woman. She was humble, soft-spoken, and made you feel so happy to be in her presence.

The way my grandma suffered in her last years, her son should be charged with murder. He sold the family land—

180 acres in Texas—and that broke my grandma's heart. He starved my granny, keeping her in the house with black garbage bags on the window. I would call her, and she would revert back to the time when people couldn't go outside after dark because the slave master or the Klan would get them. I told my mom, "You better book a flight and go check on your mom."

We went to visit my grandmother, and my uncle had changed my grandma's house deed to his name. How could that happen when he has siblings? That was crazy. Also, he was a lawyer, so he had the town people fooled into thinking we were crazy. The police and Elderly Protective Services did not investigate to check on the status of my grandma. They believed the evil man. My uncle stole her retirement checks from her deceased husband, her social security, and did not pay any utilities. The house was paid for... he canceled the house insurance. But he was a lawyer, so that is why he knew what to do. He even gave my granny meds she wasn't supposed to take. She was supposed to take 3 pills, but he gave her 7, and it made her crippled, fragile, and bedridden.

Greed will make people do some crazy things. He even forged a document saying that my grandmother was married to him so he could get all of her assets. The family acted like they were afraid of him. I wasn't. He didn't scare me, but I was the grandchild; it wasn't my fight. I gave my mother $24,000 to get a probate lawyer to help us with visiting my grandma in the hospital and hospice, and to get everything changed into all of the siblings' names.

Chapter 5
A Journey Through Family and Betrayal

My great-grandmother's house is no longer there since we lost the land. The only thing we have are mineral rights. My mom and I drove to Texas, went to the court records, and added all the heirs of my grandma on record so that the mineral rights could be divided fairly. Also, the oil company is Exxon. The lady said once the royalties build up, they would send a check to my grandmother's house, and we would have to appoint someone to get the moncy and divide it. I said it would be me since I paid to get everything in motion.

Nine years later, a check came. My uncle, who stays in my grandma's house, received the check and sent it to his brother in California. My uncle says he deposited the check, but the bank said it was no good. How in the hell can you deposit a check and the bank tell you that? The check was for $36,000. I just thought I'd get my money back. I didn't get a dime.

Then, another check came. My uncle gave the check to his niece, and she sent it to my uncle in California. That was about $26,000. People act funny when money is involved. It's not about the money because I always get money tenfold; it's the principle. I helped them, and they gave my mom and me nothing.

When some family members needed a place to stay, my mom opened her doors for my uncles, aunt, cousins, and even the uncle who killed my grandmother. He took over my room for two years. Since he wouldn't move, my mom moved out. She left him, and he moved to Louisiana to stay with his mother—a grown man who doesn't want to pay bills. He gets disability, though, and he would give his brother a pill. His brother, who had a stroke, died. One thing before my uncle Mozell died: he apologized to me and my mother for what his son did to me when I was little. He asked for my forgiveness, and after he apologized to my mom, he died 2-3 days later.

Then, my crazy uncle Kenny did the same thing to his mother. That is crazy! I didn't know my family was evil about greed. Money makes people do some of the strangest things. I am an only child, so I can't relate or understand how people can treat one another like that. I have the patience of Job and a kind heart to help everyone in need. I realize sometimes when I help people, they take advantage and don't really need my help; they're just trying to use me, to get something out of me, and think I'm an ATM always having money to give them.

I am drained. No more free rides, no more paying phone bills, utility bills, buying food, taking them to the store, giving money to wash their clothes, or buying them clothes. I have endured so much pain from my family. I even told them I was disowning them for inviting the one person I couldn't stand and not having the common decency to let me know, to give me a heads-up about who all was coming. Then when I react the way I do, I am wrong. No, they are wrong because, even though it's my mother's house, why would you make me feel uncomfortable? That shows me that they don't care about me, respect me, or value my feelings. So, I know how to distance myself and not be bothered by any of them. It is just that my child doesn't get to know her family because they mistreat me like this.

I always thought maybe I was born into the wrong family and my real family is somewhere out there in the world... educated, drama-free, stress-free, and waiting on me to find them so they can embrace me into where I belong. I used to ask God why the people who are supposed to be my family, who should accept me, love me, and be there for me, treat me the way that they do. I'm still waiting for God to give me an answer.

I love to read, travel, drive across countries, go to museums, festivals, concerts, and explore new horizons. I am thankful for all the good times, but I dislike the way they made me feel. I would always be told that I think I am better than them. I went to college, but it took me 10 years because of my brain injury. My cousin said it's going to take 50 years to get a degree. Well, I earned it, and she still, to this day, doesn't have anything but a high school diploma. I've never thought that... or acted that way. I guess my being around them makes their inner demons come out.

Chapter 6
Letting Go of Family Pain

I always get hate, envy, and jealousy from them. I am not jealous of anyone. I always encourage, help, and am there for them when I can. Now that I am older, I realize you can have a family without being blood-related. I have friends that I have known for years who treat me like family and have never done any of the things my family has done to me. I am antisocial sometimes and don't want to be around anyone. It's easier for me to distance myself when I feel unappreciated or judged. It's my way of keeping my peace and positive energy—not fighting or cussing anyone out. I don't want my child to see me act a fool and be out of character.

Over the years, I have struggled with relationships because I have trust issues and sometimes fear the new person is out to get me. It all is rooted in the beginning with my abuse and family trauma. My mother is very critical of me and praises my cousins for their accomplishments, not me. She even looks at me like she is disgusted or something. Now that I have my own daughter, I don't need her approval for anything. I work hard for my child. I make sacrifices to be a better parent for my child.

When I was going to college and had just begun graduate school, my mother would criticize me for having my child at daycare for 10 hours. She wasn't paying for it and couldn't watch her. She made me feel discouraged, and I dropped out of school. I have been bouncing from job to job, trying to make a decent living for the past 7 years. I don't like struggling and living paycheck to paycheck. I don't qualify for housing assistance or food stamps because my income is higher than the poverty level. I struggle to make ends meet sometimes, but I will do side jobs like DoorDash to take care of my responsibilities. I am not knocking people who get assistance; I understand the struggle is real. I am simply saying that I don't qualify for it.

My child's father is finally working, and I would have thought he would help out. I was wrong because that isn't the type of man he is. If I have to work three jobs and my parents watch my child for me, I will make enough money to take care of myself and my child. I have been homeless twice—when I was pregnant and when my child was nine. I didn't tell anyone, especially my family; they wouldn't have helped me, just talked about me. I don't like people in my business.

I have moved to California, Texas, Louisiana, and back to California with my child. I had the desire to move away, so I just packed up and went. I didn't stay long in any of those places, and my family says that I just waste money like it grows on trees. I do what I want whenever I want to and don't need their approval on how to live my life. I fly out of town to see a concert because that's what I want to do. I've always been a free spirit—maybe a gypsy in another life. I feel you only live once, and I can't live for others; I just do me.

On my journey of self-healing and making inner peace with myself, I've learned people will always talk about me, no matter if I am doing good or bad. It used to bother me that I would be the topic of discussion with some of my family members. A wise person once told me not to worry if people talk about you—only worry when they're not talking about you, LOL. Life is too short. We can't pick the family we are born into, but we just have to deal with and embrace the craziness that we have. Learn to love them, forgive them, and appreciate the good times with the bad. Under no circumstances should anyone have to deal with abuse, and if the slander becomes too much, you can always love them from a distance.

I wish one day I could meet my ancestors that my granny told me about.

Chapter 7
Finding Peace in Family and Self

I want to take a moment to reflect on just how much my family has shaped who I am. My grandmother, mom, dad, and uncles all played incredibly important roles in my life, each of them leaving a unique imprint that has guided me to become the person I am today. The life lessons they passed down, their strong sense of morals, and the guidance they provided have all been instrumental in helping me grow into the woman I am. Every day, I strive to embody those values, to be a better mother for my daughter, and to pass on the wisdom I've inherited from them.

Losing my grandmother was a turning point for our family. She was the glue that held us together, the one who ensured we stayed connected and grounded. Since she passed, I've felt the painful shift in our family dynamics; it's as if the bond that once united us is now frayed and brittle. I've made efforts to mend those bonds with my cousins, hoping to restore some of that closeness, but it's not always easy. Some of them bring too much toxicity into my life, and it's more than I can handle. I've come to realize that I need peace more than I need family drama. I'm not someone who enjoys constant arguments or endless tension—I'd much rather keep my distance, stay calm, and protect my peace of mind.

Still, I miss the sense of unity that my grandmother cultivated. I often wish that my children could experience that warmth and closeness with their extended family, to grow up with those connections and shared memories to cherish. Sadly, the reality is different, and many of my own painful, even traumatic, experiences are tied to the wounds my family has inflicted. Over time, I've learned how to manage that pain and keep it from controlling my life.

As I've grown older, I've discovered the importance of truly appreciating and loving myself. I've become my own support system, something I never thought possible in the past. I used to feel like I needed my family's approval or support, but now I know I don't. I focus on what matters most—doing what I need to do for my child, making choices that bring me happiness and fulfillment, and living life on my own terms.

www.ingramcontent.com/pod-product-compliance
Lightning Source LLC
LaVergne TN
LVHW041005150826
845672LV00002B/879
9798895698044